THE SMART SINGLE MOM DATING GUIDE

A Single Mother's Dating Guide to Find a Date and Seek for True Love

Jane Davis

Copyright © 2019 by Jane Davis

All Rights Reserved

Disclaimer:

No part of this publication may be reproduced or transmitted in any form or by any means or transmitted electronically without direct written permission in writing from the author.

While all attempts have been made to verify the information provided in this publication, neither the author nor the publisher assumes any responsibility for errors, omissions, or misuse of the subject matter contained in this eBook.

This eBook is for entertainment purposes only, and the views expressed are those of the author alone, and should not be taken as expert instruction. The reader is responsible for their own actions.

Adherence to applicable laws and regulations, including international, federal, state, and local governing professional licensing business practices, advertising, and all other aspects of doing business in the U.S.A, Canada or any other jurisdiction is the sole responsibility of the purchaser or reader.

CONTENTS

Introduction vii

Chapter One: Sex And The Single Mom 1
   1.1 Single Moms Should Not Be Excluded 1
   1.2 Where Do You Belong? 3

II. The Non-Committal But Sexually
Active Single Moms...6
   Keep The Relationship Away From The Kids 7
   Do Not Get Carried Away.......................................8
   Be Protected..9

III. The Serious Relationship And Sexually Active
Single Moms...9

Chapter Two: Why Do You Want To Date?......... 11
   2.1 All The Right Reasons 12

1. Love.. 12

2. Companionship... 13

3. Sex 14

4. The Kids Love Him 14

    2.2 It Is Never About Marriage 15

    2.3 It Only Gets Better 16

    2.4 Touch Of Optimism 17

Chapter Three: Are You Ready For This? 19

    3.1 Date Readiness Tips For Single Moms 20

I. Free Yourself From Emotional Turmoil
Of The Past 20

II. Know What You Want 22

III. Make Out Time For The Date 23

IV. Never Underrate Yourself 23

V. Enjoy Yourself 24

    3.2 More Tips To Follow: 25

Chapter Four: Conquering Your Fears 26

    4.1 How Soon Is Too Soon? 27

    4.2 Do Not Look Back 30

1. Being Uncomfortable With Your Body 31

2. Doubting Your Abilities 32

    4.3 Overcoming Your Past 34

Chapter Five: What About The Kids? 37

    5.1 Dating Does Not Make You
A Bad Parent 38

    5.2 How Soon Should He Know
About My Kids? 38

    5.3 Telling The Kids 39

    5.4 Ensure You Meet The Kids' Needs
Before Leaving 40

Chapter Six: Finding The Right
Man For You 42

    6.1 Tall, Dark And Handsome 43

    6.2 Seducing Mr. Perfect 46

1. Be Yourself And Love Yourself 46

2. Flirt 47

3. Have A Life Going For Yourself Besides Him 47

4. Get Him To Do Stuff For You 49

5. Smile And Laugh More Often 49

6. Be Excited To Meet His Friends 50

7. Dress Well 50

8. Be A Good Listener 50

9. Maintain Eye Contact 51

6.3 What If He's Got Kids 51

Chapter Seven: Introducing Your Date To The Kids 54

   7.1 Before You Introduce That Man.................. 54
   7.2 Make Sure Your Man Is Ready To Meet The Kids... 55
   7.3 Let The Venue For The Introduction Be An Informal/Public Place.............................. 56
   7.4 Ease Your Date Into The Experience........... 56
   7.5 Be Yourself At All Times............................... 57
   7.6 Reassure Your Kids 57

Chapter 8: Making It Work 59

   8.1 Behind Every Successful Man 59
   8.2 Silver Lining... 61

Do's 62

   8.3 Happily 'Never 'After 66

Conclusion... 68

INTRODUCTION

Dating and single moms are more or less like a zig-zag line. There is simply no consensus. For some single moms, dating is a no brainer. Others just want to date to have fun and satisfy their cravings, while others just want to get into another relationship and get married, again. This set of single moms just want someone to help to share the burden of raising up the kid(s). Another set exists, who just live their life of single motherhood by chance. This set doesn't go all out to do anything about their status. To them, anything goes. If a man comes, he comes, if he doesn't, they are fine.

The society has played its role as well when it comes to single moms and dating. A lot of societal misconceptions exist about this topic. The society has placed an imaginary scale system for single mothers. Most of these misconceptions, to me, are very much bizarre. To society, it is not morally right for a single mom to go on dates or have sexual relationships. She can only do these if she is planning on getting married. Anything outside of wedlock is wrong. These dates and sexual freedom, if enjoyed by single moms will mean less time for her responsibilities as a mother. Personally, I don't feel single moms should be judged this way. We are humans and we have cravings too. Give us a break. Please. Why should we be judged for our sexual choices?

One other problem most single mothers wishing to start off new relationships is the kid's reaction. Would they approve their new boyfriend? Would they like him? Such questions make some single mom hide their relationships from their kids. I would say if you have entered a new relationship and you have gotten to a level where you feel it can work out well, tell your kids in time. Never go into a relationship that will never be beneficial to your kids. Always have their time. They are your first priority.

Another fear harbored by single mothers who would want to go on dates for the benefit of having another relationship is the fear of it not ending well. If the relationship is all good and looks like it's going to become a success, and the kid(s) have become used to him and then boom, it crashes. What would be the reaction? How will the kids feel? These things could give such kids a bad impression about love and relationships. What pitfalls need to be avoided to handle these issues? Will the relationship be sustained?

All these uncertainties put many single mothers off when it comes to dating. Some prefer to date for the fun of it, with no obligations or responsibilities. Those who intend for their relationships to last longer and lead to healthy marriages thus have to plan ahead and check those boxes before deciding.

This book seeks to **help single mothers to navigate through the tides of single parenting and dating. How to balance the act, how to make the right choices, how to avoid failing again.** It comes with tips, personal experiences, and expert advice. It has tried to allay the fears faced by single mothers for dating and tries to put them in a better position of decision making.

As a single mother of three lovely children, I have come across some of these experiences and will share them here, hoping it will help readers. Single moms rock at dating. Conquer your fears and rock that boat. See you soon.

CHAPTER ONE

SEX AND THE SINGLE MOM

1.1 Single Moms Should Not be Excluded

Scientific facts abound that tell about the very many advantages of sex. In case you don't have an idea of such scientific revelations, let me run them down for you in a jiffy.

- Sex lowers the blood pressure
- When you have sex, the rigors of a stressful day are released.
- Sex improves the immune system
- Sex improves your sleep
- Sex makes you happy...why not?
- Sex is beautiful and should be enjoyed.

- As a single mom, your sexual experience is greatly reduced and in some cases, non-existent. But who says that a single mother should be left out of having and enjoying a beautiful sex life. There is no rule book that a single mom **MUST** remain celibate. It is by choice. If a single mom decides to be celibate and not enter into any relationship, sexual or not, it is all well and good, as long as she is comfortable with it and remains happy. If she decides to do otherwise, it is also all well and good, as long as she can handle the situation and does not allow it get out of hand, and her kid(s) are not affected negatively by it.

Being a single mom gives room for a lot of self-discovery and freedom to explore new things. You pay your bills yourself, wear the clothes you want to wear and are independent. Your only obligation is to yourself and your children. Society, however, feels that single mothers having sex out of wedlock is wrong. She should be married. Her time should be dedicated totally to her children and thus give no room for sexual activities, except she intends to marry again. I totally disagree with this notion. Everyone deserves to be loved and being a single mother should not be a barrier to this. Your child or children's needs should come first no doubt, but you should be happy while performing your role in their lives. You deserve to take care of yourself as well. As a single mom, after your children's needs, your needs are next. Sometimes you are all alone by yourself and feel the need to be loved again. These feelings crop up once in a while and your hormones and will continue to crop up. It has surely been a while since you hit it in the sheets since your last relationship and you feel the need to get loved up, told sweet words and cuddled.

1.2 Where Do You Belong?

How you handle this period depends largely on if you want to have a relationship as a single mom. And if you want to have a sexual relationship, what kind of sexual relationship do you intend to have? In my experience, I have discovered that single moms can be divided into three groups when it comes to being sexually active. The way you handle yourself sexually as a single mom depends on the group you belong to. This is because your decisions and how you react to your sexual feelings depends on what you have decided to do. Here are my groups:

I. The No-Sex Policy Single Moms

These categories of moms are majorly widowed moms or moms who were too emotionally marred by their past relationship that they have blocked off any relationship of any kind with the opposite sex. For widowed moms, this stance may be due to their attachment with their late partners and the bond they shared with them. These categories of single moms focus all their energy on their kids, family, and friends. Dating is a no-go area for them, and sex too. They feel nothing can top that and are willing to keep to themselves no matter what. Another reason for this stance could be age. Widowed single moms who feel too old to engage in relationships may also zero off from going into relationships. Single moms scarred from their past relationship may also decide not to engage in any relationship of any kind. They focus all their energy on their careers and their kids avoiding anything that would lead to any relationship of any kind. Sometimes with time, this hard stance could change, especially if they meet someone who can somehow make them let go of such ill feelings towards men. Another reason can also be attributed to strong religious inclination. Whereby such single moms believe it will be against their beliefs to have sex outside of marriage. Whatever reason is behind their policy, these women are very much comfortable keeping to themselves.

An experience comes to mind here of my friend and widowed single mom, Betty:

"Patrick's death really hit me hard. We had been married for 6 years and we courted each other for 5 years before saying I do. He was everything to me. We had a son who we named Benjamin.

When Patrick died after a heart attack, my whole world collapsed. I was not expecting much at that time, but death gives no warning, does it? After his death, I had to heal. And I needed to be strong for Benny. He is just four you know. He is the one thing Patrick and I created and I am going to make sure I do all for him. So, I don't need any man. I am independent and have a good career. That's enough. Benny is my world, he is Patrick's gift to me. So, no manner of cravings can lead me to another man's arms. To me, that would be unfair to Patrick. My vibrator can handle my cravings if it needs handling".

Wow! The vibrator part got me!

II. The Non-committal but Sexually Active Single Moms

These single moms are those that remain sexually active while being single moms but do not enter into deep relationships. The relationships they keep are just for sexual benefits and it ends there. Many single moms do practice this form of sexual relationship. While it may suit their needs and satisfactory levels good, there needs to be some caution here. If you are in this category or intend to go into this category of sexually active moms, be sure to ensure that you take the following steps:

Keep the relationship away from the kids

If you have young children who do not understand these things, it is best to keep your sexual activities away from your home. If it has to be in your home, do well to ensure that the kids are not home. If they begin to see your partner frequently, they may become to get used to him and you may not want this, except you want to go further with the relationship. Hence it is best to avoid sleepovers in your house or frequent visits. If your kids are in their teenage years, you won't want them to have the impression that sleeping with random men who you are not attached to is a normal thing, so you also have to do well to keep it away from them. More mature children, who are nearing adulthood or are adults are the best to deal with things as these. They know how the world works to an extent and understand that you have your needs. So, telling them of your sexual relationship is okay. Just know how to breach the topic with them and explain the terms of the relationship with them. When you tell, make sure you detail their reaction. The way a female child reacts will be different from that of a male. Listen to their opinions too. However, if you feel they may feel uncomfortable with it, it is best keeping it away from them. The relationship is only beneficial and is not leading to anywhere, so it can be cut off at any point in time.

Do not get carried away

If you are in this sort of relationship, you have to know where to draw the line. Do not become too into each other that you want it to become a relationship that will be more than what it is.

Remember you got attracted because of sexual appeal and not because you have things in common. I repeat, know where to draw the line. He is your lover and not your boyfriend. You only call him when you are craving, not when you want someone to talk to or when you have personal issues. If you misplace your feelings, you run the risk of being heartbroken soon.

Be Protected

It is best to protect yourself when indulging in sex with a lover. It is also important to keep only one lover at a time. Having multiple sexual partners can be deleterious. Protect yourself against pregnancies and STDs. You won't want to bear a child out of sexual satisfaction. That scenario won't do you good trust me.

III. The Serious Relationship and Sexually Active Single Moms

These categories are the single moms who are in a relationship that is serious and has obligations. They hope to find fulfillment in such a relationship and are hopeful it has a happy ending. These single moms go on dates in order to find the right man to suit their needs and are willing to also accommodate her kids. Single moms in this category or who consider dating will find these books really helpful. In this kind of relationship, care should be taken to ensure that the partner is all in for you and has your best interest at heart. Make sure he is determined to make this work and accommodate the kids before giving in to sexual demands. This will make it hurt less if the relationship does not work out.

We are done with my little category of single moms based on sexual needs. I hope you found it helpful and educative. Let us move on to the next one, shall we?

CHAPTER TWO

WHY DO YOU WANT TO DATE?

Parenting is one heck of a challenge. Coupled with being a single parent. That's the height of overwhelming, you might say. Extremely exhausting. It is only natural to have the occasional thought of how easier it would be if there was a co-parent. One might tend to feel intimidated by those thoughts, even feel guilty for having them. Atta girl, there is nothing to be ashamed of. We are only humans after all. And more importantly, a woman. As much as we are genetically engineered- as I'd like to say- to share the burden, you need to understand that THAT alone is not a telltale reason to jump onto a relationship with the first guy that pops up. You need to be sure and get your **whys** straight first because remember, every slightest decision you take also affects the kids.

As a single mom, you need to be clear about what you want in life, as well as where you are headed.

That said, there is clearly zero tolerance for hasty, spur-of-the-moment decisions. So, you've got eyes for this handsome new colleague that has been making passes at you since you stumbled into each other on the elevator. You've gone on a few dates, and it's been awesome.

2.1 All the Right Reasons

Suddenly, you find yourself thinking he is the next best thing after chocolate. Not so fast lady! Before you take that relationship to the next level, you need to slow down and ask yourself why you want to date. Feelings come and go. In the same way, these feelings can be influenced by just about anything, not just his handsome face or comeliness. It could as well be infatuation, hero-worship or just a desperation birthed by years or months of loneliness. Here are 4 common reasons why a single mom might want to date;

1. Love

Love is inevitable in a relationship if it's going to work. In order to go into a relationship with someone, there has to be some level of love, and this love has to be mutual on both sides. A common occurrence among single moms in love is that they tend to have this feeling of guilt like they are being unfair and selfish to the kids. And this plays out terribly in most cases as they spend every waking moment with the guy talking about the kids, in order to convince themselves that they've got the kids at heart always, hoping it would relieve the guilty feeling. Everyone deserves to be happy, and if being with him makes you happy, it is nothing to feel guilty about. Go for it. You owe yourself at least one date night which is solely about you without the kids to worry about. It does not make you selfish. Just be sure he feels the same way about you- And you've got a great baby sitter. Winks.

2. Companionship

One of my biggest turn-offs is seeing a woman who can't live happily without a man. That brings desperate and clingy to mind. Being a single mother has made me realize how much

I could achieve on my own. You are stronger than the world knows. There is this supernatural confidence and energy that comes with being independent and having your kids around, and I am so loving it. But there is always a need for companionship. I mean, that amazing dinner gown can't be your date to the ball, right? Neither would the leaky sink fix itself.

3. Sex

This seems pretty obvious, but it goes beyond finding someone that makes you scream in bed.

Okay, good sex makes a relationship work 80% of the time. Fine, 85%. Sex, however, is not all you would be doing in the relationship. There are bills to pay and friends to meet and functions to attend. So, if you both are sexually compatible, but socially worlds apart, you might want a rethink.

4. The kids love him

Again, here is another obvious one. "*Dress a lion in Santa's costume and the kids would jump on him still,*" says 29 years old Anna, a single mother of three. The good thing is, for the kids to love him, it means they have met him. Meaning he is not some random stranger, but someone you trusted enough to meet your kids. I mean. You can't introduce the kids on a first date, right?? You just don't do that. So, dear singles, before introducing that guy to the kids, be sure he is good enough for them, and you too. Who knows, they just might like him, and boom! You just might have something going.

2.2 It is Never About Marriage

Have you ever wondered why some women find joy in waving their wedding ring on your face? Well, it is because you let it get to you and they know it. They want it. Marriage is not always the almighty panacea. Being a single mother, there is a 70% chance that you have once being married, so why stress it. Unless she is waving that ring for you to observe the 3000 carats diamond and patronize her jeweler, you shouldn't be concerned. That is never enough reason to pressure the next guy that comes your way into proposing. Neither is the fact that you just got an invitation to your ex's wedding.

It does not matter how many proposals you have had to turn down, or how bad you felt about being the only one of your colleagues that showed up at last night's dinner without a date. If you go into a relationship for the wrong reasons, it always backfires. Get your priorities right.

2.3 It only gets better

You might not have as much time as you had like to go out and meet people. But let your limited time not be a barrier. Remember, you are single. Have fun, have a Friday night out, meet people, get drunk, kiss a stranger if you must. Laughs. Anything to stop you from feeling left out and pressurized. Once you feel you are suffocating, it is time to let loose. But act responsibly though. Never do what you wouldn't want your kids doing at that age. Trust me on this though, worse than an irresponsible mom is a sulky, grumpy, bitter, frustrated mom with cobwebs down there. Do what you love doing so you do not end up bitter and frustrated and take it out on the kids and others around you until you drive off everyone that loves you and ruin your chances of finding love. No one loves a bitter old woman. What is the worst that could happen? Having an actively functioning social life going for you reduces your chances of falling for the wrong guy. How? You might ask. Well, the more you go out, the more people you get to meet, the more places you see. New faces, new characters, new cuisine, new... Whatever it is that is in vogue. You are less likely to consider it a glimpse of heaven when you experience these things with a prospective date. That way, there would have to be other strong points about him to impress you not just the excitement and his choice of Turkish wine. Plus, you are not wanting. And what do you know, you are having the time of your life. Be my guest!

2.4 Touch of optimism

This eBook is not channeled towards making me seem like the perfect single mom who always knows the right thing and go for it every time while castigating all the single moms faced with having to take a more realistic and challenging approach when it comes to dating. We cannot turn a blind eye to the set of single moms out there who are faced with arranged marriages, crazy matchmaking friends, or just plain old " I'm in a tight corner and he's super-rich, so why not. Besides he is handsome and treats my kids well". Okay, these are terrible reasons to go into a serious relationship, but given the situation, when faced between the deep blue sea and a hot bowl of chocolate, predeceases, I'd choose the chocolate a hundred times over. But mind you, if what's on the other side of you and the blue sea can be likened to the devil, it is a no-no. Flee!

Do not forget, you must have a clear picture of why exactly you are going into that relationship.

Once u could give yourself an honest answer with a clear idea, go ahead and rock the dating boat.

CHAPTER THREE

ARE YOU READY FOR THIS?

Having made the decision to go on a date, which I feel is a good one, it is right that you also know that there are things you need to be on the lookout for to be sure you really want to mingle. Dating is really not A, B, C and for single moms, it could only get tougher. All those times of being alone and independent really take away some of your wills to date. No wonder most single moms stay off dating, bringing up excuses which sometimes can be laughable. For you single moms that want to date, it is good to be sure you really are ready, so that you don't ruin your date, and then join the bandwagon of people who feel single moms suck at dating. I have here some tips based on expertise and experience that will help single moms out there, who are willing to enter into the dating scene to prepare their minds adequately for this bumper ride.

3.1 Date Readiness Tips for Single Moms

I. Free Yourself from Emotional Turmoil of the Past

If you are a single mom whose last relationship ended in a very unpleasant manner, it is best to give yourself enough time to completely heal before venturing into another relationship. It will be a very awkward situation if you go on a date and end up talking about your past relationship or making references to it every now and then. It will surely point you out as an emotionally unstable person and give all the wrong signals to a potential date. If you have experienced a terrible relationship, it is best to partake in activities that will relax your mind and refresh your spirit for new experiences. Do not sulk over such things. I know it's easier said than done, but if you want to have another relationship, it is necessary that you do not let your past relationship bring it down before it has even set flight.

Evelyn, a single mom, with two kids shares her experience:

"My relationship with Mark was a very beautiful one. We did everything together and I longed for him even if he was a second gone. We never married, but we lived together and I had two children for him. When I discovered that he had a wife in another part of the country, I was so heartbroken that I almost killed my self. My friends really saw me through during this period and with time I was okay, or so I thought. After some time, I was encouraged to go on a date, and I did. Well, it turned out to be a bad idea as I was not fully over Mark. The innocent dude said some things, which were harmless but reminded me of what Mark used to say, and I totally lost it.

I went berserk! I wasn't ready for that experience I guess".

So, you see, if you are not sure of yourself, don't go on that date. Live the past out of it...for now.

Try to know more about your date and see if you have a chance with him rather than talking about your past relationship.

II. Know what you want

Before you go for that date, make sure you set out your preferences. Hey, not what you are thinking. I don't mean the 'he must be tall, he must have sexy eyes, a cute smile' and all that. Those are good, but not as important as your innermost preferences. What kind of man do you want to have at this point in your life? Do you want a man who will be close to the kids or not? Do you want a single dad? Do you want a man that will always be with you all the time or the once in a while kind of man? It is good to have some preferences or needs in place that will suit your desires. Even if changes have to be made to your preferences, ensure that you are happy with it. Don't settle for less just because you don't want to be alone. Don't say because you want a man that will be good with the kids, then you date someone who never has the time for you or pays attention to your needs. Whatever choices you make, always ensure that you are happy and well catered for. Remember that after your kids, you are your next priority. Never forget that.

III. Make out time for the date

Imagine you have planned a date and all is set, and you suddenly remember that you have to take Phil, your 6 years old son to see the dentist. You obviously will have to call off the date and that is never going to be cool. A lot of single moms have encountered this problem, and this is caused by poor planning. If you are planning a date, ensure it does not clash with your primary responsibilities for your kids, as you will always have to choose them over any other thing. So, make sure you have the kids stay over at a relative's place, or on vacation so that you don't cut short your chance to meet a new beau. Plan ahead of time. It is really important.

IV. Never Underrate Yourself

Single moms sometimes feel they are no good and will not be attractive to men. 'Who cares about me, am all worked up and unattractive!" Hmmm! Give yourself a break lady. You are beautiful. If you have the desire to date, freshen up, have a nice bath, put on that sexy dress and rock the scene. Never look down on yourself, you are the mother of those beautiful kids remember. Be confident in yourself.

V. Enjoy Yourself

Before going on a date, make it a priority to plan to enjoy yourself no matter what happens. Do not worry yourself about things you can't control or bug yourself over whether the date will be okay or not, and if it will lead to anything meaningful. Dear, you spend your whole day babysitting and running after those little ones, don't spoil this one romantic night with such thoughts. Just go with the flow. If your date is weird, laugh it off with drinks. If he is hot and digs you, dance with him. Whatever you do, don't be boring. Enjoy your day to the fullest. There is no need for worrying over things and risk having a boring night.

3.2 More Tips to follow:

Make sure you have talked to your planned date many times over the phone and have built some sort of connection before agreeing on a date. You may risk ruining a date if you know very little of each other before a date. Do not release valuable information to a potential date without first meeting them and knowing who they really are. Have it at the back of your mind that not all dates are going to work. A failed date is not a reflection of yourself. Do not give yourself any undue pressure. Relax.

I hope you have found this tip helpful. As always, they are not a 100% guarantee of success. You know yourself better than anyone else. Whatever you do, make sure you are happy and most importantly, that your kids are not neglected.

CHAPTER FOUR

CONQUERING YOUR FEARS

The first time I had to go out on a date after the divorce, I literally had to sneak out of my house and sneak back in afterward. Plus, it was the shortest date ever in the history of dates. And for some reason, I had to insist he dropped me off four blocks away. Creepy!

That was three months after the divorce. I had just gotten full custody of my two beautiful boys. All I had in my head that night was "what kind of mother would people think I was?". The whole dating scenario felt all wrong to me. Not even my two weeks of premeditation could prepare me for the remorse I felt afterward. Now, was it too soon? Was I with the wrong guy? Or was it just me? Thankfully, it was a casual hookup and no feelings were hurt.

Two years down the line, I think of that night and cannot actually believe that had been me.

Society has a bad-ass way of knocking a belief into your head so much so that you start living it. Neighbors, family, friends, they all contribute to it and are the leading culprits influencing how you choose to thread. If you enjoyed dating before you had kids, why not after? For several reasons, you may be stuck thinking about what kind of example you would be to your children if you went all out. How do you expect your kids to ever loosen up and come to you for dating advice if they have never seen you date? Or talk to you about sex if they think you are celibate. Perhaps you are just scared of getting hurt again. None the less, steering clear of dating completely is never a way out of those walls of doubts. You need to face it head-on and conquer those fears.

The good news is "**you are not alone**".

4.1 How Soon Is Too Soon?

Healthy sex life and romance are normal, and being a single mom should not take normal away from you. Many single moms make the mistake of believing that being a mother, and single automatically triggers the "nun" Button. Celibacy is never a criterion to judge how good a parent you are. You may fear what the world might think about you if you give in to your cravings. You resort to sneaking around, denying yourself or getting your dildo to work. Give me a break. If you feel like having sex, why not? It does not make you a nympho. It does not put you on the stakes for the world to condemn. Having an emotional connection with the opposite sex, in fact, makes you a happier mom. And being sexually fulfilled and contented is a bonus. The more the merrier. If the world is going to condemn you over anything, it should not be about dating or how often u choose to have sex.

One recurring question among single moms is: "How soon can I start dating?" And I always give the same honest answer- YESTERDAY. If you are lacking emotionally, it rubs off on the kids. It makes no sense to sacrifice your entire happiness on the altar of being a good mom. That is just a framed way of saying "I am Scared to love again". Widowed single moms especially tend to withdraw into a shell for the most part. Likewise, victims of rape. Getting to love and trust again becomes a tough nut to crack. And the idea of dating seems alien and absurd. Letting go is key and requires months, even years of actual trials. I once had the privilege of meeting 19 years old Sophie. A jolly and cheerful fellow though she was, I had a hard time believing that the cuddly, cute, little angel she held was hers. In her words;

"Danny is my world. I love him with all I've got. Getting raped at sixteen is something I hate to think about, but it gave me Danny. For two years of my life, I wanted the world to just stop. I wanted all guys to just puff away. I had given up in love and relationship and sex. Especially sex".

Remarkably, I can boldly say that Sophie is one of the strongest women I ever met. At nineteen, she has been able to successfully combine college and parenting and still work part-time in a coffee shop. *"One look at her and you'd never guess she's ever had it rough,"* says her college boyfriend Matt. You don't need superpowers to overcome whatever doubt or fears you might have, u just simply have to accept your sexuality and embrace it.

4.2 Do Not Look Back

Now that we have gotten comfortable with our sexuality, any doubts concerning whether it is okay to go into a relationship now are finally out of the way. So, let's do what they do. If we are on the same page, you would likely be thinking now, if it would be that easy to get dating once you decide to date. Well, that is good. That is exactly the thought I want you to have. There is a lot involved in the dating game, and motherhood, unfortunately, does not make it any easier. Coupled with career prospects, the time factor, and oh no! There's the extra belly fat to worry about. Having second thoughts? Don't turn back now. Let us conquer them one at a time.

☐ **Conquering your insecurities**

I could think of a million reasons why you might want to fiddle out at this point, but your insecurities should not be one of them. If Thomas Edison had dwelt upon his near-deafness, he probably would never have had invented electricity. Insecurities are a major hindrance to dating as it kills both self-esteem and confidence. Sadly, single moms are mostly susceptible to this self-worth depriving false thinking. Such insecurities include, but are not limited to:

1. Being uncomfortable with your body

Nothing sucks worse than not being comfortable in your own skin. Challenges related to how or what we think about our physical appearances are usually the most disturbing, most destructive yet, easiest to fix. Those after birth stretch marks might look distasteful and ugly to you, but trust me, that would be the last thing on his mind when he's taking off your clothes. I get amazed sometimes when I hear mothers complain about their figures when to me, they look smoking hot! Having a baby could have added a pound or two to your perfectly cut figure, but that does not rule you out of the dating list. If you think that because of your extra pounds, no guy would ever want you or be attracted to you, think again babe. Your aura of confidence and a great smile work the magic twice better than sexy looks. Besides, who says extra flesh isn't sexy??! And if what you want is to fit into your prom dress again, cool. You might not look as sexy as you used to, but nothing hitting the gym twice a week wouldn't fix.

2. Doubting your abilities

All mothers are extraordinary. Well gladly, that makes we single moms superhumans. You work, sometimes put in extra hours to keep your job, you take care of the kids, read them bedtime stories, drive them to school, pick up. Yet you make out time to visit and keep in touch with family and friends. And now there's dating. How often do you get tempted to chicken out of a relationship because you fear u cannot meet up to his expectations? What with having limited time to offer him. My take is, if he knows you are a parent, he would understand that your time is not yours alone. I am certain he won't mind the delays in meeting his friends or last minutes' change of plans. And if he does mind, perhaps he is not the right one for you. You are extraordinary. You can have it all. Do not live in constant fear of defaulting.

- Should I tell him about the kids?

What if it scares him away? Well, that is his loss. No matter your fears, you must tell him as soon as possible that you are a mom, before you get too involved. He deserves to know and if he is not cool with that, he would have lost a super amazing, extraordinary superhuman.

- What if the kids do not like him?

Truthfully, the kids can not like every guy you go out with. But it is your obligation to know why they don't. It is important however that your kids approve of anyone you plan to have a more serious relationship with, that would be long-term and could lead to marriage. Younger children or toddlers are easier to deal with in this regard as they constantly tend to seek out a prominent father figure in their lives. While you are thinking "please like him" with your fingers crossed, they will be more of- "yeaaahhh!! I've got someone to take to me bring your dad to school day tomorrow". Older kids, however, are a workload. Seeing him as a threat, you would be the replacement of their real dad, and a possible usurper of your love for them. That is where the challenge lies. This should not stop you from telling them about him anyway because sooner or later, they would have to know. The earlier you realize someone cannot fit into your children's lives, the easier it would be for you to drop the charade and move on. Just trust your intuition.

4.3 Overcoming your past

Chances are, every single negative thought and feeling you have now, that is affecting your dating decisions were built up by your past relationships, consciously or unconsciously. Years upon years of listening to your ex tell you how clumsy you are, would leave you believing you are the clumsiest person on earth. This mindset could last even years after the divorce, if not forever. Single moms who left verbally abusive relationships more often than not live with low self-esteem and zero self-worth for the most part of their lives because they have grown into believing the verbal abuses are just honest opinions about themselves, who they are and what they represent. Never let your past relationship stop you from living your life to the fullest because of fear of being scorned all over again. See a therapist if need be. Just anything to let go of the past.

Having residual feelings for your ex is another sad story. Focus all that love and energy on the kids and your career and you would be over him in no time. That should work. Having unresolved feelings may not entirely stop you from seeing other people, but it will certainly make you feel bad about not being able to reciprocate your new partner's feelings and eventually you decide to drop the "I'm not cut out for this" boulder. What better way of saying "I want you out of my life because I can't love you and I fear this would backfire". Using your ex as a magical dating scale could leave you single for life. Not every guy out there could be as tall as he was or as handsome or kiss as good. A lot of single moms are guilty of this without realizing. You are done with your ex. Stop making him a standard with which to judge other men. And please, do not fall in the habit of comparing your new partner with your ex. Be open to new love. Give dating a chance.

CHAPTER FIVE

WHAT ABOUT THE KIDS?

Your fears have been conquered. You have decided to hit the dating scene, but then you remember the kids again. You begin to feel guilty all of a sudden. What if they need me while I am gone? What if someone gets hurt? And then will I be able to cope with them if this gets serious? Oh! I am leaving them to go be with someone else. Baby girl, your fears are only natural and should crop up. How you deal with these fears is going to define how successful your single mom dating life will be. For most single moms, the dating scene is filled with a mix of fear and excitement. And adding the kids into the picture may well make you despise your dating life. You may also be afraid that your date will shriek at the mention of your status. Fears, fears, and fears all over. Let's get all these fears, away shall we?

5.1 Dating does not make You a Bad Parent

The belief that as a single mom, when you go out to date has taken away some valuable time from your kids is erroneous and should not be accepted. When single moms date, it helps them find another way to be happy and not totally dependent on their children for happiness. Hey there! Don't get me wrong. I am not saying your kids should not be happy or that you should not be happy. I am saying that your happiness is also important, and your kids would also like you to be happy. You trying to connect emotionally with someone else out there does not mean that you are going to have no time for your children. It takes planning and understanding from both parties involved. It's all about finding the right balance. That is the word, balance. While on a date, do not get carried away and forget that you have children at home. Except they are on vacation though.

5.2 How soon should he know about my kids?

Single moms also fear to let their dates know about their children for fear of it pushing them away. Well, as I have said before, it is the man's loss. Baby girl, do not be ashamed of your status. Your children are your jewels and whoever wants to be in your life should see them as such. So never hide this fact. You only run the risk of getting serious with someone who may not finally be cool with it when you finally tell him. Don't leave a lie, be honest.

5.3 Telling the Kids

Single moms also grapple with the thought of telling their kids that they are seeing someone. Most experts agree that you tell your kids only when you are sure that the relationship is very serious and has a direction. Then you can tell them and then do the introduction (we will talk about this in later chapters). I am no expert, but I feel the matter of telling the kids about your date depends on the maturity level of those kids and their willingness to accept it. If you are dealing with very young kids like mine, you do not tell them just yet until you are sure your date and you are very much serious and ready for the next level.

As for teenagers and much older children, you don't want them to find out about your relationship from elsewhere. These kids have a way of finding out such information. It is right that you tell them as soon as your relationship begins to hit off. When telling them, do not put it in a way that suggests that you are seeking their approval or forcing them to accept your partner or your right to date. Rather, you are doing it because you value them and see their importance in your life. The conversation should be honest and the kids should be made to feel comfortable and with the knowledge that they are your first and foremost priority. Set them an example of rightful relationships, love for family and support for one another.

5.4 Ensure you meet the kids' needs before leaving

Before you step out of the house on your date, it is right that you ensure that you have made enough plans for your children's wellbeing. Leave them in very good hands, who you really trust to handle them while away. I personally feel your dating plans should happen when your kids are away on vacation or away in school. That way, you wouldn't have to worry too much about them hurting themselves while you are out. Provide everything that they will need while you away. You wouldn't like to be on a date and suddenly remember that you forgot to make lunch for them or did not turn on the Wi-Fi before leaving. You are going to meet a host of angry faces when you return home, and you wouldn't enjoy that trust me.

All single moms who are actively dating have their way of taking care of their children's needs while away. You know your kids more than anyone else. Devise the plan or tactic that best suits them. Enjoy your date dearie.

CHAPTER SIX

FINDING THE RIGHT MAN FOR YOU

The idea of the right man is relative, and also dependent on the individual in question. While I may want an average height, tanned, down to earth athlete with an Italian accent, a lighter, tall, corporate Englishman might be what it takes to leave you in jelly bits. It takes more than looks though to make the perfect man, he should also have the same drive, same passion and some vision to succeed. It is such a big world we live in with lots of people, if you are going to meet that right man, you need to exhaust your options. And I mean, join dating sites, social media platforms, go partying, hit the gym, do charity works, go clubbing. You never can tell where you might run into him. I often encourage single moms to date more people at the onset of their dating game so they could leave their options open and see who comes clean at the end. That way, even when you are not ready to commit, you get to date without getting too involved with one person. However, there comes a time when you have to commit and get exclusive.

6.1 Tall, dark and handsome

Looks alone does not define a man, but it is the first thing we see even before noticing his $20,000 Rolex wristwatch. Check an average woman's wish list for her dream man, and you would see tall, dark and handsome topping the list before smart, funny, enterprising, resourceful and 100% into women in my case. As a single mom, looks do not quite cut it for me. I am past my teenage fantasies at this point, as you should be. I am not asking you not to have a wish list, sure, the guy has to be attractive enough to attract you, but there are other things to look out for before saying yes when he pops the big question;

- Does he share your feelings for him?

- Are you compatible? Do you have a lot in common or is it just sex?

- Does he love your kids enough to take up the daddy role?

- Are you 100% sure, that you are not just a pass time for him?

- Is your relationship well defined or do you guys just have a "thing"? This aspect especially should be taken seriously lest you fall victim. You need to know where you stand in his life. You cannot be thinking of taking the relationship to the next level whereas to him, you are just fuck buddies.

- Is his professed love genuine or is it just obsession?

- Does he have kids of his own?

- How does he behave with other people when you guys are out? This goes a long way in telling, the kind of man he really is behind all those masks of "trying to impress you".

- How does he treat other kids? Does he love kids generally? Does he have records of child abuse? This is a telltale sign of how he would treat your kids. He can't claim to love your kids when he doesn't care for other kids. Loving kids is kind of an 'all or none' thingy.

- How successful is he in his career? Is he just a thinker or a doer as well?

- Does he value your opinion? Does he make it count?

- Does he have a history of domestic violence? Learn from his past relationships without seemingly being nosey.

If your reply to any of the questions above is not satisfactory enough for you, or you are indecisive about anyone, then maybe it is time to move on keep searching till you find your Mr. Right. Unless of course, all you are after is just a casual hookup that is all about sex and nothing more. This way, he should not even be meeting your kids to start with.

6.2 Seducing Mr. Perfect

I bet you are wondering what this is about. Relax, I'm not going to ask you to let your hair down, put on some kick-ass Victoria's Secret lingerie over those drop-dead stiletto heels and rock that blood-red dripping lipstick and shove your butts in his face. Okay... you might need the

lipstick. Winks.

Finding the picture-perfect man is one thing, but actually winning him over body, soul, and spirit is another. After all, Mr. Right has to stay right. Here are some proven tips, compiled by me, to help you stay tuned.

1. Be yourself and love yourself

Being plastic only wins you popularity, and that definitely has no place in your love life. You do not have to go out of your way to impress him. If he is going to love you, he will love you for you, and that you include a single woman who has kids of her own. Be just that and watch the magic unfold.

2. Flirt

Yeah, that's right. Your Mr. Perfect may not be the first to get attracted to you. You would actually have to work to get him to notice you. Make the handshake linger longer, throw in a touch of that vanilla spray to compliment your dressing and get close enough for him to perceive it. Use that red lipstick you haven't touched in years. Blush with a shy smile when he catches you staring (and make sure he does), it gives a hint of innocence, and the perfect combination of independent and innocent is priceless. Know when to draw the line though, you do not want him getting the wrong signals.

3. Have a life going for yourself besides him

And by that, I don't mean one that is centered around the kids. You should have other conversation boosters besides how Junior hates onions or how Sally drew up a painting of the Mona Lisa. Let him see that you are fun, let him know that you've got friends to actually hang out with on Friday nights. Something else, don't just sit around awaiting his calls and don't call no matter how much you get tempted to pick up the phone and hit that speed dial unless you actually have something important to say. He knows you are a single mom, chances are people around him would have fed him a million reasons why he should not date a single mom, telling him how demanding you would be, and he would be looking out for those signs even if not consciously. If you let him call, he would feel like he is the one calling the shots, feel less choked up and admire you more for being an independent, kick-ass single mom. And this might seem wrong, but you do not always have to be available. You could decline a date night offer every once in a while, so you don't seem like a wanton woman awaiting his next bid. But be careful so all your excuses, stories and reasons won't always be about the kids. There are other reasons to skip a date that has nothing to do with Declan's fight at school.

4. Get him to do stuff for you

Men love it when you get to ask them for help. It tickles their ego. It gives them the feeling of being a provider and a protector. You might know how to replace that electric bulb like the back of your hands, but it doesn't hurt to play the novice sometimes and let him be the hero who saves the day. But do not overdo it to the point you start seeming needy and demanding. It becomes a turn-off. The logic is being less independent without being too dependent. So, know when to be either one. I mean, a woman who could fix her flat tires herself in an emergency situation would impress just about any man.

5. Smile and laugh more often

This makes you seem less rigid and more approachable. And gives you extra beauty points.

6. Be excited to meet his friends

Be fun, be open. Pay attention to them. Seem interested, like you actually want to know them. Add to the conversation, ask questions. Try remembering their names too. He will love you more.

7. Dress well

Dress as u want to be addressed, but whatever you wear, be sure it is attractive. I want to be addressed as a picture-perfect, morally sound mom, but I won't be caught dead wearing baggy sweaters on ankle-length flay skirts. Just saying.

8. Be a good listener

Do not always do the talking. Be a good listener too. Know when to listen. Sometimes he just wants to rant away undisturbed and hear your honest opinion only when he is done talking. That could put you off sometimes I know. You have to listen to his unspoken words as well. His silence doesn't always have to mean he's mad at you. It does not always have to be about you. Something else might be bugging him, and he'll talk when he's ready. He may just be angry that the Cleveland Cavaliers lost a basketball game.

9. Maintain eye contact

Personally, this works for me 100% of the time, right from my adolescent years. It could be because there's something about my eyes (which happens to be my unique selling point), or because it simply gives the impression of "you've got nothing to hide" and also you are sending an unspoken signal, a sort of nonverbal message with some mystery to it. Whatever the case might be, it works!!

6.3 What if he's got kids

Omg!! He's got kids of his own. He is a single dad! Big deal. I am currently in a relationship with a single dad, and it has been awesome all the way. The best I have ever had. I am almost tempted to ask every single mom out there to add "Being a single dad" to your Mr. Perfect wish list. And you'd be glad you did.

There is one thing you have to contend with though; Expect resistance from his kids, just as yours might have resisted him at some point. It is like a kid's thing. You are there to steal their dad and their mom's place. Do not think they would just welcome you with open arms. It falls on you both as parents to allow your relationship with his kids to develop gradually and naturally. They will come around once they stop seeing you as a threat. So, do not go about changing the family traditions no matter how lame you think they are, rearranging furniture's, changing the living room layout or suggesting alternative parks to hang out for a family picnic. It helps to present yourself as their friend, and gradually, they'll let you assume any other position you might want. Never force it though. Another way is to let them meet your own kids. There is a general saying that "with children all over the world, we are always friends". So, true. When Fabian told, me it was time to meet his daughter, I almost had a panic attack. I had heard so much from him about his rebellious 15 years old angel. I thought at once that she wasn't going to like me, and I wasn't wrong. Fab tried to get us to spend more time together. It took us several visits to her dance class and nights of having her fix herself in between us at the movies before she could even say my name. And when she met Cal and Declan, her attitude changed towards me. She became less sulky. Now she even asks me for dating advice. And she offered to babysit my kids on my last birthday! She has not fully accepted me, but we are progressing.

CHAPTER SEVEN

INTRODUCING YOUR DATE TO THE KIDS

When is the right time for you to introduce your date to the kids as your boyfriend? Many single mothers always battle with this question when they get excited about their new beau. They then begin to have raging battles about the acceptance of each party (kids and lover) of one another. What if it goes all wrong? What if and what if? A single mom's mind is always filled with these and many more. Let's get down to the issues and try to tackle them.

7.1 Before You Introduce that Man

Hey there! Just before you go about introducing any man to your kids as a potential suitor, lover or father figure, you must have attained a level of certainty about him and be very sure that you two are cut out for a relationship and it's going to be meaningful. If you are into erratic relationships and indulge in changing men, it is not advisable to keep introducing each man to your kids. This is not going to be helpful to them and they may begin to see you as an unstable mom. Therefore, ensure that your man is ready to be in a relationship with you for real before your kids meet him. It is very necessary.

7.2 Make Sure Your Man is Ready to Meet the Kids

Men can develop some sort of cold feet when it comes to things as these. It is only natural. Do not pressurize him to getting to know the kids, it is natural if he feels that way. You would also feel that way if you are seeing a single dad and have to visit his kids as well. Give him time. However, if he begins to linger too long and bring up unnecessary excuses, it is a sign that he is not committed to you and your kids. Hit the exit button baby girl.

7.3 Let the Venue for the Introduction be an Informal/Public Place

The venue of the introduction should be an informal and playful or fun setting, where everyone can express themselves and the kids can also participate fully. The meeting should be short, sweet and relaxing. There shouldn't be too many long conversations. I suggest you have a fun activity planned beforehand that involves everyone. It calms the mood and allows for easier communication.

7.4 Ease Your Date into the Experience

Do not pressurize your date into making statements or do things while there, it could make him feel awkward and uncomfortable. Allow him to gain control of the situation and use his intuition except when it is very necessary that you lead him on. Do not have too many expectations from him. Men like to be in control of things and this is no different.

7.5 Be Yourself at all Times

Do not pretend or show yourself in another light. Do not make the kids do what they are not used to all in a bid to please your date. Let him see you for what you really are. There is no need to behave in an inferior manner. It will even make your kids dislike your date as they would feel threatened and at a loss due to his presence. Let everyone relax and be themselves.

7.6 Reassure Your Kids

Make your kids understand why you need to date, especially if they are older kids. Make them know that you would be a happier mom having a partner, assuring them you are not going to be splitting your love between them and him. Your love is only being widened and he is no threat. If your kids still see their real father, it is right that you make them understand that your date is not taking his place in their lives and that their relationship with their father is not affected by your date. Be honest at all times with your children. Inasmuch as you want to be happy, never neglect them.

CHAPTER 8

MAKING IT WORK

You have probably been out of the dating boat for a while now. And all this is seeming strange to you. Dating all over again, going through all that trouble of dividing your attention, then the butterflies when your phone rings and it's him calling. It is like being a teenager all over again, only then, you did not have these little ones. With all that is at stake now, how do you make this work without getting worked up? Dear mothers, fasten your seat belts as I take you through this ride.

8.1 Behind Every Successful Man

It takes two to tango, but inevitably, one has to be the better dancer. Relationships are like fireworks, it takes a little spark to set it off. Once set off, the resulting explosion can be beautiful when viewed from above, but if it sets off before reaching its destination heights up, it becomes a beautiful disaster. Why not try to prevent the disaster from happening?

The little things we do in a relationship are just tiny sparks. If they ignite in the right pairs, the relationship would be a smooth ride. Little gestures like thank you, a simple pat on the back, a knowing smile, even having a shared word could go a long way. You know how far you have come to have your man, why not put in a little extra work to keep him? Be the secret to his success, be a wise woman and build your relationship. He should not do all the work involved in sustaining the relationship. It does not hurt if you spice it up as well. Take him out on dates, get him presents, plan a surprise romantic evening with him, encourage him, send his write-ups to the publisher if you think they are great even while he's still contemplating because he is uncertain. Be spontaneous. These things count. He would love and appreciate these gestures as much as you would when he does the same for you. He needs you to do them even though he won't ask. Be the secret behind his smile, his happiness, his laughter. Be the source of his new-found confidence, and his love for you would multiply, his family would appreciate your presence in his life. Walk him through his hard times and he would be better for it. Devote your attention to him. Do not get me wrong, care for your kids above all, but your partner should not feel Left out no matter what.

8.2 Silver Lining

It is no secret that rosy relationships require active work to stay rosy. Ignoring faults, ignoring smutty remarks from his kids, overlooking annoying comments, reaching a compromise basically. Amidst all of these, you keep going because you know there is light at the end of the tunnel. If you plan a long-lasting relationship with him, how long do you think you could keep overlooking those faults? Do you plan to endure forever? How long do you suppose it is going to be before you explode? Say you eventually get married, how long would you be able to tolerate his habit of leaving his shoes lying around. It might seem trivial now, but think picking up one shoe from the stairs, and the second of the pair from the kitchen floor, every morning for the next twenty years. Still, care to overlook that? Like all other aspects of life, dating as a single mom has certain guiding rules which I am going to summarize as do's and don'ts.

Do's

- **Honesty**: Be honest in your relationship at all times no matter what you fear it might cost you. The prize of dishonesty is a hundred times worse when it backfires. And it always backfires.

- **Establish trust**: Win his trust and let him earn yours. If you do not trust him, suspicion sets in. And please, for the sake of your kids, you need to trust him enough to know what he can and can't do. Trust him enough to know your babies are safe with him.

- Make a conscious effort to love even when the butterflies fade away.

- Commit emotionally to your partner through good and bad times.

- **Be spontaneous:** It helps in relationships to be unpredictable. Do unexpected things that will thrill him. Spontaneity keeps the initial excitement alive and adds spice to the relationship.

- Carry your kids along so they do not feel Left out. Know that they remain your number one priority, so all your decisions, in one way or the other should revolve around them.

- Effective communication is a must for a relationship to work out. Talk as much as possible in a day, see your partner at least three times a week if you live apart. Communicate your doubts, communicate your wants, your preferences, your likes and dislikes, your fears, your thoughts.

Keeping things bottled up does not make them go away. They simply pile up in your heart until you cannot take it anymore. And the resulting explosion is terrible.

- **Show your love explicitly**: Both to your kids and your partner. Never assume they already know you love them. Tell them constantly, you never know who might need a little reassurance. Your partner loves hearing how much you love him as much as you do. Hold hands, share loving gestures, public display of affection is a bonus. kiss him for no reason, lean onto him at the movies even if the movie is not that scary.

Don'ts

- Do not constantly suggest a breakup each time the going gets rough. It soon loses its meaning and falls on him as empty threats just like any other music.

- Never compare him to your ex

- Do not disclose everything that transpires between you two to other people. The whole world doesn't have to know all your problems.

- Do not take too long to resolve a relationship crisis or disagreement.

- Do not try to compete with his ex.

- Do not see his kids as competition.

- Try as much as possible not to break promises. Be a woman of your words.

- Do not compare your relationship with that of other people.

- Do not play the distance game just to prove your point. Your kids might need him even if you are determined to prove you don't.

- Do not keep secrets about you or the kids.

- Do not make your partner and the kids feel they are competing for your love.

- Do not stick around if you feel you or your kids are being manipulated by him. Never, I repeat, never remain in a manipulative relationship. It affects the kids negatively and plays out for them badly in the long run.

8.3 Happily 'Never 'After

Your new-found relationship is not always going to be a bed of roses. There will be fights, quarrels, bad habits to contend with and what have you. Despite all odds, you both need to reach a compromise and work your way around certain hitches. Understanding each other is key. You need to figure out the next step now that you are in a settled relationship. Know each other's expectations. The next step in the relationship should be a mutual agreement between you two, and it should be clear. Whether marriage is in the picture in the nearest future is something you both should decide in order to know how involved you are going to be. You do not want to involve someone in your kids' lives and get them to love him, only for you guys to break up, and then bring home an entirely different guy a month later. Do not confuse the kids. They already suffer the loss or absence of one father, don't make them go over it over and over again. It is like re-living the hurt. Whether you guys are just going to keep dating, or get married eventually is up to you. Just try not to let the kids suffer for your decisions. Try as much as possible to live as one big happy family.

CONCLUSION

There is no rule that states every single mom must start dating. Neither is there a law declaring when to start dating. There is no judgment against you if you decide to remain single, provided your reasons are not borne out of fear. Getting off a bad marriage might seem a good reason to never date again, but need I remind you that dating isn't a prelude to marriage. It is a way of having fun, meeting new people, satisfying your curiosity. It does not have to be about seeking commitment.

This book has tried to show you that you shouldn't let your happiness suffer because of misconceptions and societal beliefs. Go out there and cast your nets. However, never let your relationship never affect your connection with your kids.

Ensure that you date a man who satisfies you sexually, emotionally, and loves your kids as well. If you have any fears, conquer them before you set sail. This eBook is a typical guide to overcome those fears and should be your constant companion until you are a hundred percent sure that every doubt is gone, and every fear conquered. There is no room for doubt and indecisiveness in your relationship. You can't afford that luxury anymore now that you have those little angels to protect.

My sincerest gratitude goes to you for reading this book and I do hope it's been helpful in getting you right back on track. The knowledge shared here has helped thousands of single moms out there in settling conveniently into single motherhood without being emotionally detached. During the course of writing this book, I have had the opportunity of meeting several other single moms from different spheres of life, and they all agree on one thing, the fact that their romantic life cannot be denied. Some way, the cravings would always come, there is need to have a satisfying romance every now and then, and what better way of getting it than putting yourself out there as a prospective date partner.

Dating as a single mom is a beautiful thing, but not when it's at the expense of your children. If you have successfully read this book to this point, you are well on your way to a successful dating adventure. No amount of reading, however, can give you that dating experience you crave. You need to get back out there and get dating. So, you are single, and a mom and you want to date but don't know how to go about it, I've got you covered. Let me see your smile. Dating as a single mom! Why not?

Thank you for reading " The Smart Single Mom Guide ".

If you enjoyed this book and found this book helpful, please consider leaving a review, even if it's only a few lines; it would make all the difference and would be very much appreciated. Thank you!

-Jane Davis

www.ingramcontent.com/pod-product-compliance
Lightning Source LLC
Chambersburg PA
CBHW060409080526
44583CB00012B/517